MY MONARCH BUTTERFLY
MIGRATION JOURNEY

BY JAMEE-MARIE EDWARDS   ILLUSTRATED BY MARI LOBO

PICTURE WINDOW BOOKS
a capstone imprint

Published by Picture Window Books, an imprint of Capstone
1710 Roe Crest Drive, North Mankato, Minnesota 56003
capstonepub.com

Copyright © 2025 by Capstone. All rights reserved. No part of this publication may be reproduced in whole or in part, or stored in a retrieval system, or transmitted in any form or by any means, electronic, mechanical, photocopying, recording, or otherwise, without written permission of the publisher.

Library of Congress Cataloging-in-Publication Data is available on the Library of Congress website.

ISBN: 9780756585358 (hardcover)
ISBN: 9780756585464 (paperback)
ISBN: 9780756585471 (ebook PDF)

Summary: Follow a monarch butterfly on its magnificent migration journey.

Designer: Dina Her

Printed and bound in China. 6096

Hola, amigos! That means "Hello, friends" in Spanish. I am learning new words for my trip to Mexico.

I'm a Minnesota Monarch. But my great-great-grandparents were born in Mexico. Now I get to start my journey there.

First, I'd better eat my fill from these flowers. Yum—**nectar**!

Every year, four different groups, or **generations**, of monarchs are born in North America. The first three are smaller. They only live up to eight weeks. But my group can live up to eight months, and we're bigger. That makes us SUPER! We're actually called a super generation.

SUPER GENERATION

My generation has a very important job. It's called **migration**. We live longer so we have time to do this.

Monarchs cannot live in cold weather. Like some birds, we fly south for the winter. That's called overwintering. Warm weather here I come!

I am excited but a little nervous. Mexico is far from Minnesota. I must fly more than 2,000 miles (3,220 kilometers) to get there.

When the time is right, hundreds of thousands of us take to the sky. Sometimes we look like a huge cloud of butterflies! Many people think our trip is one of Earth's most amazing natural events.

My trip will not be easy. I am small, and my wings are thin. I must protect myself from **predators** and bad weather.

I even fly across large areas of water.

But I have a secret too. Sometimes, I get a little help from nature.

My friends and I hitch rides on the wind. It helps us fly 10 to 30 miles (16 to 48 km) per hour. *WHEEE!*

Do you know what's amazing? I have never been to Mexico. But I naturally know which way to go. Monarchs from all over North America use different **flyways**. These are the paths we take on our way to Mexico.

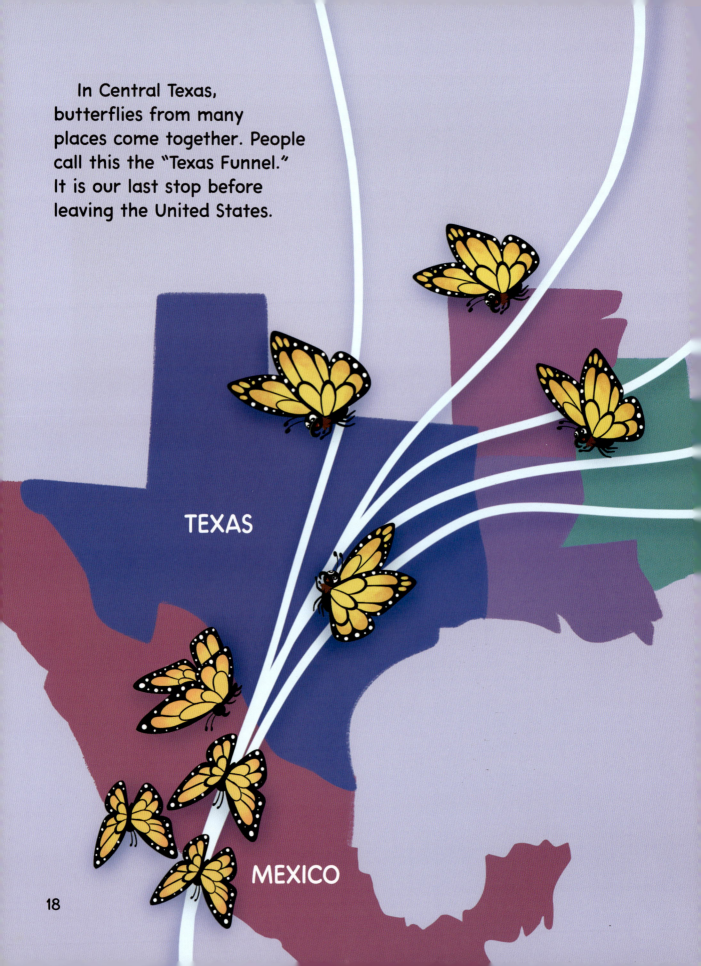

In Central Texas, butterflies from many places come together. People call this the "Texas Funnel." It is our last stop before leaving the United States.

TEXAS

MEXICO

Many people know this. They gather to see us.
They even hold **festivals** to celebrate our journey.

Scientists wonder how we know where to go. Some think we use the sun to guide us. Others think we have special senses that help us with directions. Some think it's both!

What's your secret?

We fly more than 50 miles (80 km) a day. At night, we need our rest. We **roost** in tall trees. Thousands of us gather close together. There is always room for one more.

CRACK!

Maybe not! These trees have been used by monarchs before us. They give shelter in the cool evenings.

How do you know I am the same butterfly that began in the United States once I'm in Mexico? Scientists and trained volunteers put tags on my wings. Even kids help tag us.

When I roost, the tag reports where I am.

Hola, Mexico! We are just in time for the Day of the Dead. This Mexican holiday honors loved ones who have passed on. Our wings match the orange holiday flowers.

For the next four months we sit close together in tall fir trees. We don't eat much. We live on stored energy.

In March, my friends and I travel north in search of a **mate**. My life cycle ends here, but my offspring fly farther north. Each new group gets closer to where I was born. My great-great grandchildren will be born there. And they will have their own amazing migration story, just like mine.

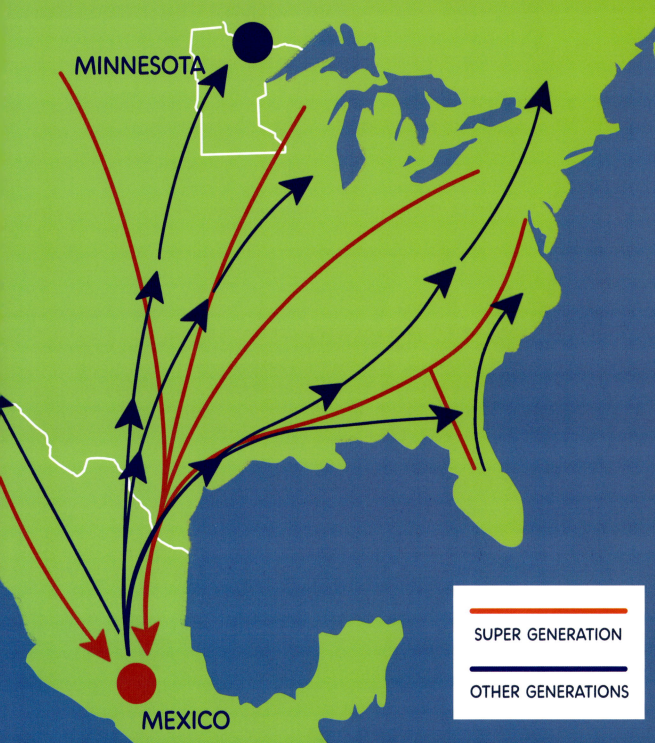

ABOUT THE AUTHOR

Jamee-Marie Edwards is an author, STEAM educator, and literacy advocate from New York City who is on a mission to ignite imagination and inspire children through creativity and education. Her experience in school health and health education has allowed her to connect with youth on various levels. As the founder of The Me I Need To Be Program, Jamee-Marie creates accessible platforms for learning in which she merges the Arts and Sciences to provide students with the opportunity to express themselves, build confidence, and gain essential skills. Learn more about Jamee-Marie at her website: maeinspireu.com

Photo Credit: MaseFX

ABOUT THE ILLUSTRATOR

Mari Lobo is a children's book illustrator and toy designer, and her inner child couldn't be happier with her life choices! She was born in Sao Paulo, Brazil, and lives in California with her husband, daughter, and two dogs. She loves all animals and would pet a crocodile if it didn't bite her!

GLOSSARY

festival (FES-tuh-vuhl)—a holiday or celebration

flyway (FLY-way)—an established air route for migratory birds or butterflies

generation (jen-uh-RAY-shuhn)—all the members of a group of people or creatures born around the same time

mate (MATE)—one of a pair that joins together to produce young; a mate is the male or female partner of a pair of animals

migration (mye-GRAY-shuhn)—movement from one place to another at different times of the year

nectar (NEK-tur)—a sweet liquid that some insects collect from flowers and eat as food

predator (PRED-uh-tur)—an animal that hunts other animals for food

roost (ROOST)—to settle in a group to rest

scientist (SYE-un-tist)—a person who studies the world around us

INDEX

Day of the Dead, 26

festivals, 19
flyways, 17

generations, 6, 8

life cycle, 28

mating, 28
Mexico, 3, 4, 10, 17, 18, 24, 26, 29
Minnesota, 4, 10, 29

nectar, 5

predators, 12

roosting, 22, 25

scientists, 20, 24

tagging, 24, 25
Texas Funnel, 18

weather, 9, 12
wings, 12, 24, 26